The
Rabbit Suit
Rescue

by Conor McIntyre
illustrated by Dee Texidor

SCHOOL PUBLISHERS

Printed in Mexico

ISBN 10: 0-15-350646-6
ISBN 13: 978-0-15-350646-8

Ordering Options
ISBN 10: 0-15-350599-0 (Grade 2 On-Level Collection)
ISBN 13: 978-0-15-350599-7 (Grade 2 On-Level Collection)
ISBN 10: 0-15-357827-0 (package of 5)
ISBN 13: 978-0-15-357827-4 (package of 5)

2 3 4 5 6 7 8 9 10   050   15 14 13 12 11 10 09 08 07

It was the day before the class play. The young woman from the costume store brought all the costumes to school. There were rabbits, mice, badgers, and owls.

"Remember," Mr. Orlowski told the children, "leave your costumes at school. They're pretty tough, but if you take them home, they might get damaged."

Joseph was so excited about his rabbit suit. He just had to take it home to show his little brother, Dan.

At home, Joseph showed Dan the rabbit suit. "Look," said Joseph, "I even have huge, furry rabbit shoes to wear."

Joseph lifted the suit above his head and pulled it on over his clothes. He hopped all around the room.

Dan laughed, "I am going to catch the rabbit!"

Joseph hopped as fast as he could. Dan ran after him and grabbed him by the rabbit ears. Suddenly, there was a ripping noise.

"Oh, no!" said Joseph. "The ear ripped off my rabbit suit."

Dad came into the room. "What's going on?" he asked.

Joseph told him what had happened. "I was supposed to leave the suit at school," Joseph said. Then he started to cry.

Dan looked worried.

"It's all right," said Dad. "I'm sure I can mend the ear. Then I'll wash the suit, and it will be good as new."

"Thanks, Dad," said Joseph. "I'm sorry."

"Next time, listen to your teacher, okay?" said Dad.

"Yes, I will," said Joseph.

The next night at the school play, Joseph hopped all around the stage. His floppy rabbit ears waved back and forth.

At the end, Joseph hopped off the stage.

"What a fantastic rabbit you were!" said Mr. Orlowski.

The audience thought Joseph
was a great rabbit, too. When he
came back on stage to take a bow,
they clapped and clapped.

Dan clapped harder than anyone else. "Joseph is really clever to hop like that," said Dan to Mom and Dad.

"Dad is really clever to mend
and wash the rabbit suit," said
Mom. "It looked just like new."

13

That night, Dad tucked Joseph into bed.

"Thank you for mending my suit," said Joseph. "Next time, I'll leave my costume at school."

"That's my smart little rabbit," laughed Dad.